SOUND™
INNOVATIONS

ENSEMBLE DEVELOPMENT
Chorales and Warm-up Exercises for Tone, Technique and Rhythm
ADVANCED CONCERT BAND

Peter **BOONSHAFT** | Chris **BERNOTAS**

Thank you for making *Sound Innovations: Ensemble Development for Advanced Concert Band* a part of your concert band curriculum. With 399 exercises, including over 70 chorales by some of today's most renowned composers for concert band, it is our hope you will find this book to be a valuable resource in helping you grow in your understanding and abilities as an ensemble musician.

An assortment of exercises are grouped by key and presented in a variety of difficulty levels. Where possible, several exercises in the same category are provided to allow for variety while accomplishing the goals of that specific type of exercise. You will notice that many exercises and chorales are clearly marked with dynamics, articulations, style, and tempo for you to practice those aspects of performance. Other exercises are intentionally left for you or your teacher to determine how best to use them in reaching your performance goals.

Whether you are progressing through exercises to better your technical facility or to challenge your musicianship with beautiful chorales, we are confident you will be excited, motivated, and inspired by using *Sound Innovations: Ensemble Development for Advanced Concert Band*.

D1217754

© 2014 Alfred Music
Sound Innovations™ is a trademark of Alfred Music
All Rights Reserved including Public Performance

ISBN-10: 1-4706-1835-4
ISBN-13: 978-1-4706-1835-3

Instrument photos courtesy of Yamaha Corporation of America Band & Orchestral Division

Concert B♭ Major

1 PASSING THE TONIC

2 PASSING THE TONIC

3 PASSING THE TONIC

4 LONG TONES

5 LONG TONES

6 LONG TONES

7 CONCERT B♭ MAJOR SCALE

8 SCALE PATTERN

SCALE PATTERN

CONCERT B♭ CHROMATIC SCALE

CHROMATIC SCALE PATTERN

FLEXIBILITY

FLEXIBILITY

FLEXIBILITY

CHROMATIC FLEXIBILITY

25 EXPANDING INTERVALS: DOWNWARD IN PARALLEL OCTAVES

26 EXPANDING INTERVALS: UPWARD IN PARALLEL FIFTHS

27 EXPANDING INTERVALS: DOWNWARD IN TRIADS

28 EXPANDING INTERVALS: UPWARD IN TRIADS

29 RHYTHM: SIMPLE METER (4/4)

30 RHYTHM: COMPOUND METER (6/8)

31 RHYTHMIC SUBDIVISION

32 CHANGING METER 6/8 AND 3/4

33 CHANGING METER 4/4 AND 5/8

8

Concert G Minor

47 PASSING THE TONIC

48 LONG TONES

49 CONCERT G NATURAL MINOR SCALE

50 CONCERT G HARMONIC AND MELODIC MINOR SCALES

harmonic minor scale   melodic minor scale

51 SCALE PATTERN

52 SCALE PATTERN

53 FLEXIBILITY

54 CHROMATIC FLEXIBILITY

ARPEGGIOS

ARPEGGIOS

INTERVALS

INTERVALS

BALANCE AND INTONATION: DIATONIC HARMONY

BALANCE AND INTONATION: MOVING CHORD TONES

BALANCE AND INTONATION: LAYERED TUNING

BALANCE AND INTONATION: FAMILY BALANCE

10

63   EXPANDING INTERVALS: DOWNWARD IN PARALLEL OCTAVES

64   EXPANDING INTERVALS: DOWNWARD IN TRIADS

65   EXPANDING INTERVALS: UPWARD IN TRIADS

66   RHYTHM: SIMPLE METER (4/4)

67   RHYTHM: COMPOUND METER (3/8)

68   RHYTHMIC SUBDIVISION

69   CHANGING METER 3/4 AND 6/8

Concert E♭ Major

76 PASSING THE TONIC

77 PASSING THE TONIC

78 PASSING THE TONIC

79 LONG TONES

80 LONG TONES

81 LONG TONES

82 CONCERT E♭ MAJOR SCALE

83 SCALE PATTERN

84 SCALE PATTERN

85 CONCERT E♭ CHROMATIC SCALE

86 CHROMATIC SCALE PATTERN

87 FLEXIBILITY

88 FLEXIBILITY

89 FLEXIBILITY

90 CHROMATIC FLEXIBILITY

14

91 ARPEGGIOS

92 ARPEGGIOS

93 INTERVALS

94 INTERVALS

95 BALANCE AND INTONATION: PERFECT INTERVALS

96 BALANCE AND INTONATION: DIATONIC HARMONY

97 BALANCE AND INTONATION: LAYERED TUNING

98 BALANCE AND INTONATION: MOVING CHORD TONES

99 BALANCE AND INTONATION: SHIFTING CHORD QUALITIES

100 EXPANDING INTERVALS: DOWNWARD IN PARALLEL OCTAVES

101 EXPANDING INTERVALS: DOWNWARD IN PARALLEL FIFTHS

102 EXPANDING INTERVALS: DOWNWARD IN TRIADS

103 EXPANDING INTERVALS: UPWARD IN TRIADS

104 RHYTHM: SIMPLE METER (4/4)

105 RHYTHM: COMPOUND METER (12/8)

106 RHYTHMIC SUBDIVISION

107 CHANGING METER 4/4 AND 3/8

108 CHANGING METER 3/4 AND 5/8

109 CONCERT E♭ MAJOR SCALE AND CHORALE

Chris M. Bernotas (ASCAP)

110 CHORALE

Ralph Ford (ASCAP)

Gentle

111 CHORALE

Roland Barrett (ASCAP)

Gracefully

112 CHORALE

Randall D. Standridge

113 CHORALE

Rossano Galante

Andante

114 CHORALE

Chris M. Bernotas (ASCAP)

Sweetly

Concert C Minor

121 **PASSING THE TONIC**

122 **LONG TONES**

123 **CONCERT C NATURAL MINOR SCALE**

124 **CONCERT C HARMONIC AND MELODIC MINOR SCALES**

harmonic minor scale   melodic minor scale

125 **SCALE PATTERN**

126 **SCALE PATTERN**

127 **FLEXIBILITY**

128 **CHROMATIC FLEXIBILITY**

29 ARPEGGIOS

30 ARPEGGIOS

31 INTERVALS

132 INTERVALS

133 BALANCE AND INTONATION: DIATONIC HARMONY

134 BALANCE AND INTONATION: MOVING CHORD TONES

135 BALANCE AND INTONATION: LAYERED TUNING

136 BALANCE AND INTONATION: FAMILY BALANCE

137 EXPANDING INTERVALS: DOWNWARD IN PARALLEL OCTAVES

138 EXPANDING INTERVALS: DOWNWARD IN TRIADS

139 EXPANDING INTERVALS: UPWARD IN TRIADS

140 RHYTHM ($\frac{5}{4}$)

141 RHYTHM: COMPOUND METER ($\frac{6}{8}$)

142 RHYTHMIC SUBDIVISION

143 CHANGING METER: $\frac{4}{4}$ AND $\frac{7}{8}$

(2+2+3)

Concert F Major

150 **PASSING THE TONIC**

151 **LONG TONES**

152 **CONCERT F MAJOR SCALE**

153 **CONCERT F CHROMATIC SCALE**

154 **SCALE PATTERN**

155 **SCALE PATTERN**

156 **FLEXIBILITY**

157 **CHROMATIC FLEXIBILITY**

58 ARPEGGIOS

159 ARPEGGIOS

160 INTERVALS

161 INTERVALS

162 BALANCE AND INTONATION: DIATONIC HARMONY

163 BALANCE AND INTONATION: MOVING CHORD TONES

164 BALANCE AND INTONATION: LAYERED TUNING

165 BALANCE AND INTONATION: FAMILY BALANCE

24

166 EXPANDING INTERVALS: DOWNWARD IN PARALLEL OCTAVES

167 EXPANDING INTERVALS: DOWNWARD IN TRIADS

168 EXPANDING INTERVALS: UPWARD IN TRIADS

169 RHYTHM: SIMPLE METER ($\frac{4}{4}$)

170 RHYTHM: COMPOUND METER ($\frac{9}{8}$)

171 RHYTHMIC SUBDIVISION

172 CHANGING METER: $\frac{4}{4}$ AND $\frac{7}{8}$

173 CONCERT F MAJOR SCALE AND CHORALE

Chris M. Bernotas (ASCAP)

174 CHORALE

Roland Barrett (ASCAP)

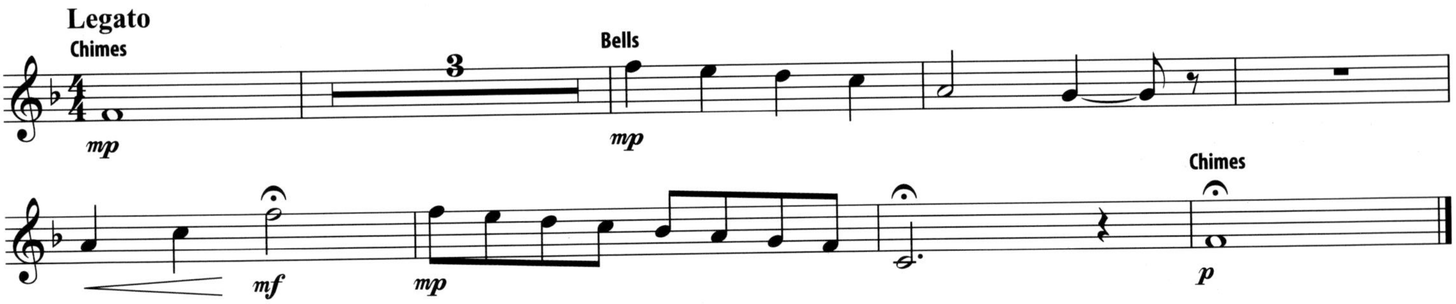

175 CHORALE

Rossano Galante

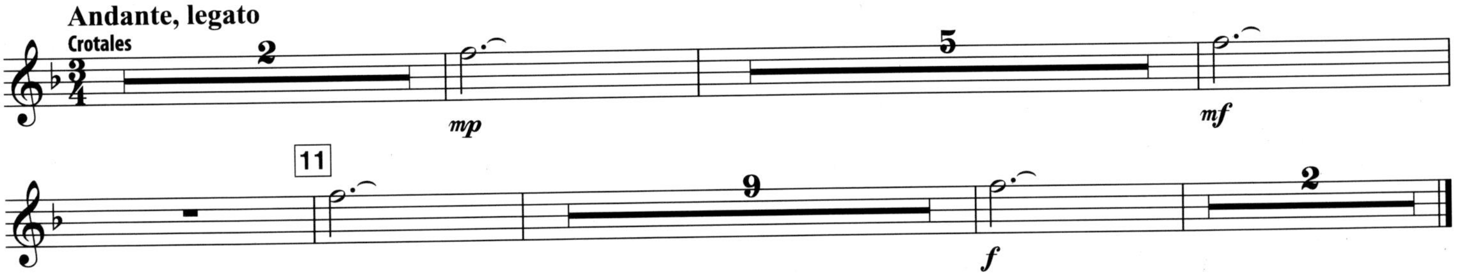

176 CHORALE

Chris M. Bernotas (ASCAP)

177 CHORALE

David R. Gillingham

178 CHORALE

Jack Stamp

Concert D Minor

179 PASSING THE TONIC

180 LONG TONES

181 CONCERT D NATURAL MINOR SCALE

182 CONCERT D HARMONIC AND MELODIC MINOR SCALES

harmonic minor scale   melodic minor scale

183 SCALE PATTERN

184 SCALE PATTERN

185 FLEXIBILITY

186 CHROMATIC FLEXIBILITY

27

187 ARPEGGIOS

188 ARPEGGIOS

189 INTERVALS

190 INTERVALS

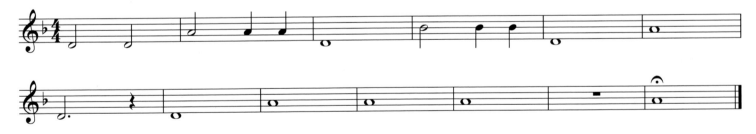

191 BALANCE AND INTONATION: DIATONIC HARMONY

192 BALANCE AND INTONATION: MOVING CHORD TONES

193 BALANCE AND INTONATION: LAYERED TUNING

194 BALANCE AND INTONATION: FAMILY BALANCE

195 **EXPANDING INTERVALS: DOWNWARD IN PARALLEL OCTAVES**

196 **EXPANDING INTERVALS: DOWNWARD IN TRIADS**

197 **EXPANDING INTERVALS: UPWARD IN TRIADS**

198 **RHYTHM ($\frac{6}{4}$)**

199 **RHYTHM: COMPOUND METER ($\frac{6}{8}$)**

200 **RHYTHMIC SUBDIVISION**

201 **CHANGING METER: $\frac{4}{4}$ AND $\frac{7}{8}$**

202 CONCERT D MINOR SCALE AND CHORALE

Chris M. Bernotas (ASCAP)

203 CHORALE

Robert Sheldon

Somber
Bells
Hard rubber mallets

204 CHORALE

Michael Story (ASCAP)

Andante
Marimba

205 CHORALE

Chris M. Bernotas (ASCAP)

Andante
Marimba
Medium yarn mallets

206 CHORALE: PRÄLUDIUM

Arcangelo Corelli (1653–1713)
Edited and Arranged by Todd Stalter

Adagio
Bells

207 CHORALE

Rossano Galante

Lento
Vibraphone
Soft yarn mallets, slow motor

Concert A♭ Major

208 PASSING THE TONIC

209 LONG TONES

210 CONCERT A♭ MAJOR SCALE

211 SCALE PATTERN

212 SCALE PATTERN

213 CONCERT A♭ CHROMATIC SCALE

214 FLEXIBILITY

215 CHROMATIC FLEXIBILITY

224 **EXPANDING INTERVALS: DOWNWARD IN PARALLEL OCTAVES**

225 **EXPANDING INTERVALS: DOWNWARD IN TRIADS**

226 **EXPANDING INTERVALS: UPWARD IN TRIADS**

227 **RHYTHM: SIMPLE METER (4/4)**

228 **RHYTHM: COMPOUND METER (9/8)**

229 **RHYTHMIC SUBDIVISION (4/4)**

230 **CHANGING METER: 4/4 AND 6/8 AND 3/4**

Concert F Minor

237 **PASSING THE TONIC**

238 **LONG TONES**

239 **CONCERT F NATURAL MINOR SCALE**

240 **CONCERT F HARMONIC AND MELODIC MINOR SCALES**

241 **SCALE PATTERN**

242 **SCALE PATTERN**

243 **FLEXIBILITY**

244 **CHROMATIC FLEXIBILITY**

245 ARPEGGIOS

246 ARPEGGIOS

247 INTERVALS

248 INTERVALS

249 BALANCE AND INTONATION: DIATONIC HARMONY

250 BALANCE AND INTONATION: MOVING CHORD TONES

251 BALANCE AND INTONATION: LAYERED TUNING

252 BALANCE AND INTONATION: FAMILY BALANCE

253 EXPANDING INTERVALS: DOWNWARD IN PARALLEL OCTAVES

254 EXPANDING INTERVALS: DOWNWARD IN TRIADS

255 EXPANDING INTERVALS: UPWARD IN TRIADS

256 RHYTHM: SIMPLE METER (3/4)

257 RHYTHM: COMPOUND METER (12/8)

258 RHYTHMIC SUBDIVISION

259 CHANGING METER: 4/4 AND 5/8

260 CONCERT F MINOR SCALE AND CHORALE
Chris M. Bernotas (ASCAP)

A

B

261 CHORALE
Chris M. Bernotas (ASCAP)

Menacingly
Bells
Hard rubber mallets

262 CHORALE
David R. Gillingham

Aggressive and forceful
Xylophone

263 CHORALE
Frédéric Chopin
Arranged by Michael Story (ASCAP)

Andante moderato
Bells

264 CHORALE
Jack Stamp

With purpose and resolve
Bells

265 CHORALE
Andrew Boysen, Jr.

Dark and dramatic
Bells

Concert Db/C# Major

266 PASSING THE TONIC

267 LONG TONES

268 CONCERT Db/C# MAJOR SCALE

269 SCALE PATTERN

270 SCALE PATTERN

271 FLEXIBILITY

272 CHROMATIC FLEXIBILITY

273 ARPEGGIOS

274 INTERVALS

275 BALANCE AND INTONATION: MOVING CHORD TONES

276 BALANCE AND INTONATION: SHIFTING CHORD QUALITIES

277 EXPANDING INTERVALS: DOWNWARD IN PARALLEL OCTAVES

278 EXPANDING INTERVALS: UPWARD IN PARALLEL FIFTHS

279 CONCERT D♭ MAJOR SCALE AND CHORALE

Chris M. Bernotas (ASCAP)

280 CHORALE

Chris M. Bernotas (ASCAP)

With motion

281 CHORALE

Roland Barrett (ASCAP)

Flowing

40

Concert B♭ Minor

282 PASSING THE TONIC

283 CONCERT B♭ NATURAL MINOR SCALE

284 CONCERT B♭ HARMONIC AND MELODIC MINOR SCALES

harmonic minor scale   melodic minor scale

285 SCALE PATTERN

286 SCALE PATTERN

287 FLEXIBILITY

288 ARPEGGIOS

289 INTERVALS

290 BALANCE AND INTONATION: LAYERED TUNING

291 BALANCE AND INTONATION: DIATONIC HARMONY

292 EXPANDING INTERVALS: DOWNWARD IN TRIADS

293 EXPANDING INTERVALS: UPWARD IN TRIADS

294 CONCERT Bb MINOR SCALE AND CHORALE

Chris M. Bernotas (ASCAP)

295 CHORALE

Stephen Melillo (ASCAP)

296 CHORALE

Ralph Ford (ASCAP)

Concert C Major

297 **PASSING THE TONIC**

298 **CONCERT C MAJOR SCALE**

299 **SCALE PATTERN**

300 **SCALE PATTERN**

301 **FLEXIBILITY**

302 **ARPEGGIOS**

303 **INTERVALS**

304 BALANCE AND INTONATION: MOVING CHORD TONES

305 BALANCE AND INTONATION: LAYERED TUNING

306 EXPANDING INTERVALS: DOWNWARD IN PARALLEL OCTAVES

307 EXPANDING INTERVALS: UPWARD IN PARALLEL FIFTHS

308 CONCERT C MAJOR SCALE AND CHORALE — Chris M. Bernotas (ASCAP)

A

B

309 CHORALE — Chris M. Bernotas (ASCAP)

Flowing
Marimba
Medium mallets

mf

f

11

mf

f

p

310 CHORALE — Robert Sheldon

Gently
Bells
Hard rubber mallets

mf

f

2

9 A tempo

rall.

mf

rall.

Concert A Minor

311 **PASSING THE TONIC**

312 **CONCERT A NATURAL MINOR SCALE**

313 **CONCERT A HARMONIC AND MELODIC MINOR SCALES**

harmonic minor scale   melodic minor scale

314 **SCALE PATTERN**

315 **SCALE PATTERN**

316 **FLEXIBILITY**

317 **ARPEGGIOS**

318 **INTERVALS**

319 **BALANCE AND INTONATION: MOVING CHORD TONES**

320 BALANCE AND INTONATION: DIATONIC HARMONY

321 EXPANDING INTERVALS: DOWNWARD IN PARALLEL OCTAVES

322 EXPANDING INTERVALS: DOWNWARD IN TRIADS

323 CONCERT A MINOR SCALE AND CHORALE

Chris M. Bernotas (ASCAP)

324 CHORALE

Randall D. Standridge

325 CHORALE: AIR, HWV 467

Georg Fredrich Handel (1685–1759)
Edited and Arranged by Todd Stalter

Majestically
(opt. woodwind and bells 1st time, brass/percussion 2nd time)

Concert G Major

326 PASSING THE TONIC

327 CONCERT G MAJOR SCALE

328 SCALE PATTERN

329 SCALE PATTERN

330 FLEXIBILITY

331 ARPEGGIOS

332 INTERVALS

333 BALANCE AND INTONATION: MOVING CHORD TONES

334 BALANCE AND INTONATION: SHIFTING CHORD QUALITIES

335 EXPANDING INTERVALS: DOWNWARD IN PARALLEL OCTAVES

336 EXPANDING INTERVALS: UPWARD IN PARALLEL FIFTHS

337 CONCERT G MAJOR SCALE AND CHORALE

Chris M. Bernotas (ASCAP)

A

B

338 CHORALE

Stephen Melillo (ASCAP)

In full glory!

Chimes

_f_

339 CHORALE

Andrew Boysen, Jr.

Slow and peaceful

Marimba

5

9

mf cresc.

13 Slower

rit.

rit.

48

Concert E Minor

340 **LONG TONES**

341 **CONCERT E NATURAL MINOR SCALE**

342 **CONCERT E HARMONIC AND MELODIC MINOR SCALES**

harmonic minor scale · melodic minor scale

343 **SCALE PATTERN**

344 **SCALE PATTERN**

345 **FLEXIBILITY**

346 **ARPEGGIOS**

Concert A Major

355 **CONCERT A MAJOR SCALE AND CHORDS**

356 **SCALE PATTERN**

357 **BALANCE AND INTONATION: MOVING CHORD TONES**

358 **CHORALE**

Chris M. Bernotas (ASCAP)

Concert F♯ Minor

359 **CONCERT F♯ NATURAL MINOR SCALE AND CHORDS**

360 **CONCERT F♯ HARMONIC AND MELODIC MINOR SCALES**

361 **SCALE PATTERN**

362 **BALANCE AND INTONATION: LAYERED TUNING**

363 **CHORALE**

Chris M. Bernotas (ASCAP)

Concert D Major

364 CONCERT D MAJOR SCALE AND CHORDS

365 SCALE PATTERN

366 BALANCE AND INTONATION: MOVING CHORD TONES

367 CHORALE

Chris M. Bernotas (ASCAP)

Concert B Minor

368 CONCERT B NATURAL MINOR SCALE AND CHORDS

369 CONCERT B HARMONIC AND MELODIC MINOR SCALES

370 SCALE PATTERN

371 BALANCE AND INTONATION: LAYERED TUNING

372 CHORALE

Chris M. Bernotas (ASCAP)

Concert B/C♭ Major

373 **CONCERT B/C♭ MAJOR SCALE AND CHORDS**

374 **SCALE PATTERN**

375 **BALANCE AND INTONATION: PERFECT INTERVALS**

376 **CHORALE**

Chris M. Bernotas (ASCAP)

Concert G♯/A♭ Minor

377 **CONCERT G♯/A♭ NATURAL MINOR SCALE AND CHORDS**

378 **CONCERT G♯/A♭ HARMONIC AND MELODIC MINOR SCALES**

harmonic minor scale   melodic minor scale

379 **SCALE PATTERN**

380 **BALANCE AND INTONATION: MOVING CHORD TONES**

381 **CHORALE**

Chris M. Bernotas (ASCAP)

Concert E Major

382 **CONCERT E MAJOR SCALE AND CHORDS**

383 **SCALE PATTERN**

384 **BALANCE AND INTONATION: LAYERED TUNING**

385 **CHORALE**

Chris M. Bernotas (ASCAP)

Concert C# Minor

386 **CONCERT C# NATURAL MINOR SCALE AND CHORDS**

387 **CONCERT C# HARMONIC AND MELODIC MINOR SCALES**

388 **SCALE PATTERN**

389 **BALANCE AND INTONATION: MOVING CHORD TONES**

390 **CHORALE**

Chris M. Bernotas (ASCAP)

Concert F♯/G♭ Major

391 **CONCERT F♯/G♭ MAJOR SCALE AND CHORDS**

392 **SCALE PATTERN**

393 **BALANCE AND INTONATION: PERFECT INTERVALS**

394 **CHORALE**

Chris M. Bernotas (ASCAP)

Concert E♭ Minor

395 **CONCERT E♭ NATURAL MINOR SCALE AND CHORDS**

396 **CONCERT E♭ HARMONIC AND MELODIC MINOR SCALES**

397 **SCALE PATTERN**

398 **BALANCE AND INTONATION: LAYERED TUNING**

399 **CHORALE**

Chris M. Bernotas (ASCAP)

Mallet Percussion

YOUR INSTRUMENT—KEYBOARD (MALLET) PERCUSSION

The keyboard percussion family includes orchestra bells, xylophone, marimba, vibraphone and chimes. Each instrument is arranged chromatically in two rows similar to a piano keyboard. Because of the different materials used, each instrument has a unique sound. Since few of the keyboard percussion instruments have been standardized in range, the most practical ranges for school use are listed below.

ORCHESTRA BELLS (also called Bells or Glockenspiel) Although some student bell kits are 1½ octaves, the standard range is 2½ octaves. The instrument is played with brass, plastic or hard-rubber mallets.

octave instrument. It is played with yarn, cord-wound or rubber mallets. Do not use wood, plastic or metal mallets!

XYLOPHONE
The most practical range is either a 3 or 3½ octave instrument. It is played with wood or hard-rubber mallets. Do not use metal mallets!

CHIMES
(also called Tubular Bells) The standard range for this instrument is 1½ octaves. It is played by striking the ridge of the cap at the top of each tube with a hammer-shaped mallet made of rawhide. A foot-operated damper pedal controls the sustain.

VIBRAPHONE (also called Vibraharp)
The standard range for this instrument is 3 octaves. It is played with yarn and cord-wound mallets. Do not use brass mallets! A foot-operated damper pedal controls the sustain.

MARIMBA
The most practical range is either a 4 or 4⅓

CARE AND MAINTENANCE

A. Use a cloth to keep your mallet instruments clean. The use of furniture polish on wooden bars should be avoided as it will leave a residue. When not in use, the instruments should be covered.

B. Mallets should be stored in a bag with your sticks.

C. Other than mallets, do not set anything on top of a keyboard instrument. It is not a table!

56

BELLS
Bells sound two octaves higher than written.

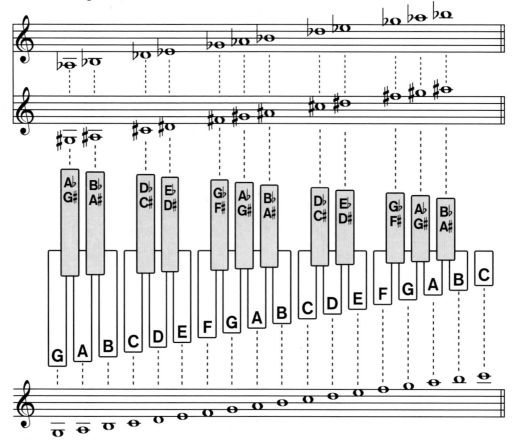

XYLOPHONE
The xylophone sounds one octave higher than written.

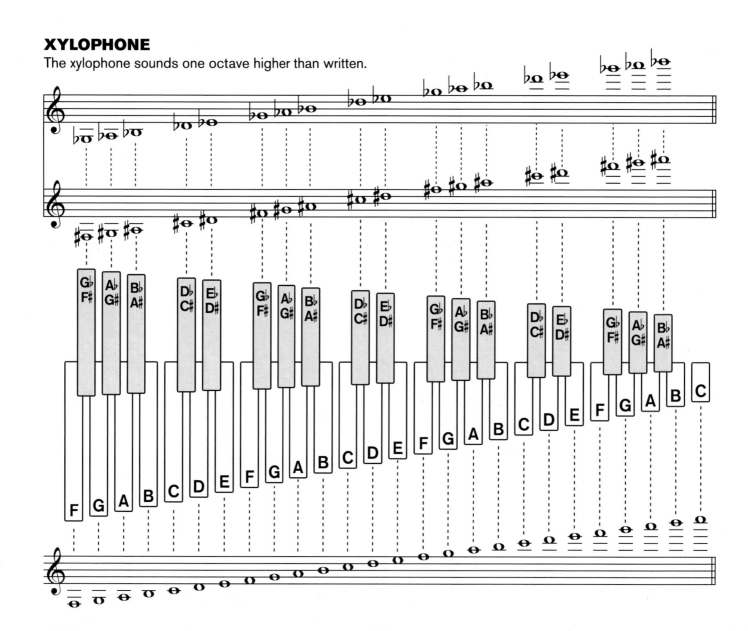